COSTUME, TRADITION, AND CULTURE:
REFLECTING ON THE PAST

Fighting Units
of the American War
# of Independence

by

Dan Harmon

Chelsea House Publishers
Philadelphia

CHELSEA HOUSE PUBLISHERS

Editor-in-Chief Stephen Reginald
Managing Editor James D. Gallagher
Production Manager Pamela Loos
Art Director Sara Davis
Picture Editor Judy Hasday
Senior Production Editor Lisa Chippendale
Designer Takeshi Takahashi

First Printing

1 3 5 7 9 8 6 4 2

Library of Congress Cataloging-in-Publication Data

Harmon, Dan.
Fighting units of the American Revolution / by
Dan Harmon.

 p. cm. — (Costume, tradition, and culture: reflecting on
the past)
Includes bibliographical references (p.) and index.
Summary: Describes various regiments and fighting units
that fought on either the American or British side during the
War of Independence.

ISBN 0–7910–5162–5 (hardcover)
1. United States—Armed Forces—History—Revolution,
1775–1783—Juvenile literature. 2. Great Britain—Armed
Forces—History—Revolution, 1775–1783—Juvenile literature. 3. Soldiers—Great Britain—History—18th Century—
Juvenile literature. [1. United States—Armed Forces—History—Revolution, 1775–1783. 2. Great Britain—Armed
Forces—History—Revolution, 1775–1783. 3. Soldiers.]
I. Title. II. Series.
E251.H37 1998   98-33502
973.3'4—dc21   CIP
                                                          AC

CONTENTS

INTRODUCTION

For as long as people have known that other cultures existed, they have been curious about the differences in their customs and traditions. Julius Caesar, the famous Roman leader, wrote long chronicles about the inhabitants of Gaul (modern-day France) while he was leading troops in the Gallic Wars (58–51 B.C.). In the chronicles, he discussed their religious beliefs, their customs, their day-to-day life, and the conflicts among the different groups. Explorers like Marco Polo traveled thousands of miles and devoted years of their lives to learning about the peoples of the East and bringing home the stories of Chinese court life, along with the silks, spices, and inventions of that culture. The Chelsea House series *Costume, Tradition, and Culture: Reflecting on the Past* continues this legacy of exploration and discovery by discussing some of the most fascinating traditions, beliefs, legends, and artifacts from around the world.

Different cultures develop traditions and costumes to mark the roles of people in their societies, to commemorate events in their histories, and to make the changes and mysteries of life more meaningful. Soldiers wear uniforms to show that they are serving in their nation's army, and insignia on the uniforms show what ranks they hold within the army. People of Bukhara, a city in Uzbekistan, have for centuries woven fine threads of gold into their clothes, and when they travel to other cities they can be recognized as Bukharans by the golden embroidery on their traditional costume. For many years, in the Irish countryside, people would leave bowls of milk outside at night as an offering to the fairies, or "Good People," believing that this would help ensure their favor and keep the family safe from fairy mischief. In Mexico, November 2 is the Day of the Dead, when people visit cemeteries and have feasts to remember their ancestors. In the United States, brides wear white dresses, and the traditional wedding includes many rituals: the father of the bride "giving her away" to the groom, the exchange of vows and rings, the throwing of rice, the tossing of the bride's bouquet. These rituals and symbols help make the marriage meaningful and special for the couple, their families, and their friends, by expressing the change that is taking place and allowing the friends and families to wish luck to the couple.

This series will explore some of the myths, symbols, costumes, and traditions of various cultures from around the world and different times in the past. *Fighting Units of the American War of Independence,* for example, will detail the uniforms, weapons, and decorations of the regiments and battalions on both sides of the war, along with the battles in which they became famous. *Roman Myths, Heroes, and Legends* describes how the ancient Romans explained the wonders and natural phenomena of their world with fantastic stories of superhuman heroes and almost human deities who could change the course of history at will. In *Popular Superstitions,* you will learn how some familiar superstitious beliefs—such as throwing spilled salt over your shoulder, or hanging a horseshoe over your door for good luck—originally began, in times when people feared that devils and evil spirits were meddling in their lives. Few people still believe in malicious spirits, but many still toss the spilled salt over their shoulders, or knock on wood when expressing cautious hope. The legendary figures of a culture—the brave explorers of *The Wild West* or the wicked brigands described in *Infamous Pirates*—help shape that culture's values by providing grand, almost mythical examples of what people should (or should not!) strive to be.

The illustrations that accompany these books have their own cultural history. Originally, they were printed on small collectors' cards and sold in the early 20th century. Each card in a set of 25 or 50 would depict a different person, artifact, or event, and usually the reverse side would offer a few sentences of description to explain the picture. Now, they provide a fascinating glimpse into history and an entertaining addition to the stories presented here.

ABOUT THE AUTHOR

DAN HARMON is an editor and writer in Charleston, South Carolina—a strategic port in the lower colonies during the American Revolution. He has written five books on history, humor, and psychology and has written historical and cultural articles for more than a score of national and regional periodicals. He is managing editor of *Sandlapper: The Magazine of South Carolina* and editor of *The Lawyer's PC,* a national computer newsletter. His special interests are Christian and nautical history, folk music, and international correspondence chess.

OVERVIEW

The American War of Independence

The American War of Independence, Revolution, or Revolutionary War, pitted "the American colonists against the British Empire." The Americans fought for freedom. The British considered the colonists "servants of the Crown" and fought to keep things that way.

That's how most people summarize the Revolution. It's natural for us to simplify things in order to understand them. It's tidy if we can learn our military history in terms of one side versus another (North versus South in our Civil War) or as one group of nations versus another group of nations (the Allies versus the Axis powers in World War II). But if we look deeper—especially, if we look at the different soldiers who fought, and why and how they fought—the issues very often become confusing and a little messy.

The American Revolution was messy enough. When we begin to study the wide array of combat units assembled on both sides, we see quickly that this was not a simple matter of "Americans fighting against British."

Most Americans *were* British (or Irish or Scottish— British subjects). In England, there was great opposition to the war, both among the citizens and in the governing Parliament. The British had no desire to fight their "American cousins" who had crossed the Atlantic simply to find new homes. In many instances, the Americans weren't just their cousins but their sons and daughters, brothers and sisters.

Likewise, thousands of colonists opposed the War of Independence. It's estimated that at least one-fourth of the settlers, called Tories, remained loyal to the king throughout the war. They aided and fought alongside the British. Often, one colonial farmer would join the American militia, while the farmer just down the road would join a local Tory unit.

So in a way the American Revolution was a civil war, with neighbor killing neighbor, brother killing brother—as in the Civil War 80 years later. An insult by one faction within a community might lead to retaliation by another, and the feud would escalate. Ultimately, angry bands on both sides committed massacres, killing those who once had been their friends—or even their blood relatives. For many future generations, into the present century, the bitterness that began during the Revolution continued in the form of family feuds.

The opposing sides weren't just "colonists" or "British." Much of the British army consisted of hired regiments from Germany called Hessians. It has been suggested that the king, George III, could not have waged war against the patriots for more than a year or two without the German auxiliary.

After France officially sided with the colonists in 1778, many French soldiers fought and died for the American cause. Some historians believe the colonials could not have won independence without the help of the French—especially the French navy, which took on the formidable British warships at a time when America's own naval power was practically nonexistent.

It was a civil war, too, among Indians, or Native Americans. Since the early settlement years, some of the eastern Indian nations had been friendly to the English. They scouted and raided along the frontier for the British Redcoats during the Revolution. Other nations were long-time allies of the French, aiding them in their clashes over territory with the British before the Revolution. Many of them helped the Americans as a way to strike back against the hated British. Sometimes Indians found themselves in hand-to-hand combat against each other—fighting to determine which group of European invaders would win the right to claim the Indians' territory!

This brief study of some of the combat units reflects the complexity of the Revolution. You'll meet British and American regulars, or "line" troops, experienced in combat but poorly paid and sternly disciplined—sometimes so harshly as to send them to the brink of desertion and mutiny. You'll meet Hessian mercenaries who fought only because they were paid. You'll meet the brave Minutemen, eager to take up arms on short notice to defend their homes and communities—but not so eager to commit to long-term service in the regular Continental army. You'll meet companies of crusty frontier marksmen on both sides, like Butler's Rangers (Loyalists) and the Green Mountain Boys (Patriots). You'll meet giant grenadiers and nimble light infantrymen, horse soldiers and artillerymen, officers and drummers.

After eight years of bloodshed—from spring 1775 until spring 1783—America won its freedom and became a separate, self-governing nation.

10TH FOOT

The British 10th Foot was a time-honored regiment, organized almost a hundred years before the American colonies rebelled. Its soldiers were seasoned in frontier combat. Just 15 years before the Revolution, they had fought against French regulars and their Indian allies in the upper American colonies and Canada.

The British had prevailed in the French and Indian War. The men of the 10th Foot, like other British soldiers, were confident they could put down the colonial rebellion quickly. They took up quarters in Boston late in 1774.

But the colonists had learned much from frontier fighting, too. They were badly disorganized, compared with the British army. When it came to the test, however, they became the Redcoats' equals on the field and in war councils. And they fought for a cause the British could not understand: freedom from the tyranny of King George.

The 10th Foot dressed differently from most other troops of the Crown. They realized that the North American colonies would be unlike other battlegrounds where armies had been subdued by soldiers of the British Empire. Maneuvering and fighting in thickly forested regions during the French and Indian War had taught them to shorten their coattails for better mobility. They also modified their hat brims. They had seen Indian warriors use crude hatchets both for combat and for daily work in the woods; hatchets in time became standard issue for British light infantry. Other royal units followed the practical example of the 10th Foot and others like it as the Revolution progressed.

The regiment was ordered home to England in 1779.

16TH REGIMENT OF LIGHT DRAGOONS

The 16th Regiment of Light Dragoons (armed cavalrymen), known as the "Queen's Own," was at the heart of fighting in Pennsylvania and New Jersey in 1777–1778. During this period the British triumphantly battered the Continental army and captured Philadelphia.

The 16th, a cavalry regiment, was raised in 1759 and was brought to the colonies the year after fighting began. It was part of Gen. William Howe's force that sought to destroy the Continentals in Pennsylvania. The campaign began with the defeat of the Americans at Brandywine Creek in Pennsylvania in September 1777. In this battle the Marquis de Lafayette, commander of the colonists' French allies, was seriously wounded.

A week later, the 16th took part in a surprise night attack on an American force at Paoli, on the Schuylkill River. Many Americans were slaughtered; the rest scattered. The "Paoli Massacre" inspired later American revenge.

Revenge of a strange nature came the following June. At Monmouth Courthouse, New Jersey, the Americans fought the British to a standstill. Oddly, the Continentals' comparatively ragged clothes were an advantage. The temperature was almost 100 degrees. Many wool-coated Redcoats collapsed on the field from sunstroke.

The patriots, meanwhile, found a lasting heroine at Monmouth: Molly Pitcher, an artilleryman's wife, who singlehandedly operated a cannon after her husband's gun crew were all killed or wounded.

The 16th was disbanded later that year because of extensive losses. Its horses and dragoons were absorbed into another regiment.

35TH REGIMENT OF FOOT

The 35th Regiment of Foot, whose soldiers wore brownish-orange facings on their red uniforms, had a long history dating to the beginning of the 18th century. This regiment served the Crown during the first half of the War of Independence. From the bloody Battle of Bunker Hill, Massachusetts, to fighting outside New York, it helped keep the Continentals on the defensive during the early years.

In the Battle of White Plains, for example, where the Continentals held a commanding position on a hill, the 35th valiantly helped dislodge the Americans. According to a report by General William Howe, the 35th formed its ranks "with the greatest steadiness" while "under the enemy's fire." Then these brave soldiers "ascended the steep hill in defiance to all opposition, and rushing on the enemy, routed and drove them back from their works."

Like other units, the 35th had drummers, as the illustration shows, and they played a vital role. Drummers served a practical purpose. They pounded march time, bonded the men together with sound, and raised them to a fever of intensity at the instant of attack. Meanwhile, the very sound of a well-drilled army approaching did perhaps more to demoralize an enemy than any other factor.

Drummers, and fifers as well, were usually boys and young men, sometimes forced into service. In most military units, they wore reverse-colored uniforms. The only weapons they carried were short swords, hung from their belts. They were expected to fight only as a last resort.

42ND HIGHLANDERS

hey were the "Black Watch," one of the most famous regiments Scotland has ever produced. Formed in 1739, the 42nd Highlanders spent their early years fighting in France and on the American continent. They were stationed back in Scotland when the American Revolution began.

The regiment arrived at Staten Island, New York, in August 1776. Within a few weeks it was engaged in the fighting on Long Island. For the next six years it distinguished itself in New Jersey, Pennsylvania, Virginia, and New York; in 1780 it briefly supported the British siege of Charleston. After one episode, the regiment received special praise from Lord Cornwallis, the British commander.

At the Battle of Harlem Heights, New York, however, the Black Watch met their match in an American unit from Connecticut led by Thomas Knowlton. When the Americans stood and fought them to a stalemate, both sides added units to the fray. At the end of the day, it was the British who withdrew—a remarkable defeat at that stage of the Revolution, when the Americans were still struggling to organize.

The Black Watch were at Yorktown, surrendering with Cornwallis's army in October 1781. By and large, though, theirs is a legacy not of defeat but of victory and glory.

The 42nd's traditional uniform, like that of other highland regiments, consisted of kilt and plaid, a rectangular length of wool used at night as a blanket. During the War of Independence, though, the unit found the army's regulation trousers and gaiters (soft shoes) more functional. They continued to wear their Highland bonnets, sometimes decorating them with feathers. Their red jackets had blue facings.

57TH FOOT

Several battles of the American Revolution have been called turning points. One was at Saratoga, New York, where the British general John Burgoyne surrendered an entire army to the Americans in 1777 and France was persuaded to join the rebel cause. At Guilford Court House, North Carolina, in 1781, the Americans technically lost to Lord Cornwallis—but proved they could inflict more damage in losing than the Redcoats could in winning; British dominance of the Southern colonies soon ended.

But one battle looms above all others as a turning point in the Revolution: the battle at Yorktown, just off the Chesapeake Bay in southeastern Virginia. That's where Lord Cornwallis in October 1781 surrendered the main British army to George Washington and his French ally, Comte de Rochambeau.

Cornwallis held Yorktown with some 7,000 British troops, including the light company of the 57th Foot. Over 16,000 colonials and their allies descended on him. Cornwallis hoped to withstand their siege until relief arrived. It never came. On October 19, Cornwallis accepted General Washington's terms of surrender. His army became prisoners of war.

The new American Congress received word of the surrender in Philadelphia (the United States capital until 1800). King George in England got the news a month later. At first, the king vowed to continue the fight; the British Parliament, however, quickly voted to end the war.

Clad in red jackets with bright yellow facings, the 57th Foot fought throughout the colonies, from Charleston, South Carolina, to Long Island, New York.

63RD FOOT

I t's a long way from Bunker Hill, Massachusetts, to Charleston, South Carolina—almost 1,000 miles. The British 63rd Foot, consisting of both grenadiers and light soldiers, fought in both places. In between, they took part in important battles in New York State.

During the Revolution, ground forces sometimes used ships for general relocation up and down the East Coast (and often battled seasickness). But for the most part, they traveled—as the unit description implies—literally by foot, often for long distances.

The 63rd was formed in 1758. In 1775, Crown forces were concentrated around Boston to confront the uprising in the American colonies. The 63rd was sent to Boston just in time to see action at what became known as the Battle of Bunker Hill on June 17, 1775.

Actually fought at nearby Breed's Hill, half a mile from Boston proper, the battle was an extremely costly victory. Under the command of Sir William Howe, the British captured the heights from rebel defenders after three bloody charges. But almost half of their 2,500 soldiers were wounded or killed before the Americans ran out of ammunition and withdrew. The British were too nearly destroyed to pursue them. A veteran of the battle remembered many years later that the screaming of injured Redcoats on the slopes was louder than the gunfire.

The 63rd served until the end of the Revolution. They fought with light muskets. Their distinctive red jackets were trimmed in dark green with white lace.

64TH REGIMENT OF FOOT

The British 64th Regiment of Foot was as intensely involved in the War of Independence as any other unit on either side. They fought at the beginning of the war, attacking Salem, Massachusetts, early in 1775. They fought near the end, far away in South Carolina.

They were a comparatively new regiment, formed less than 20 years before the Revolution, during the French and Indian War. They were sent to the rebellious colonies again in 1769. When the War of Independence began, they were part of the British army already stationed in New England. The 64th served for the duration of the war.

Gen. Thomas Gage, commander-in-chief of British forces at the outbreak of the conflict, often used the 64th as his bodyguard. The unit fought nobly at Long Island, New York, and later along the Chesapeake Bay. They earned glory—and suffered heavy losses—in the push toward Philadelphia against George Washington's Continental army. From there the "lobsterbacks" were sent to New England, then New Jersey, primarily to raid American strongholds.

In 1780 they were shipped to Charleston, South Carolina, where they helped capture the port city in one of Britain's last major victories. When Lord Cornwallis, the British commander in the south, marched his army to eventual defeat at Yorktown, Virginia, the 64th stayed behind to guard the lower colonies. They served well; near Ninety-Six, South Carolina, they outmaneuvered Francis Marion, the Continentals' legendary "Swamp Fox." They participated in the British victory at Eutaw Springs, and in late summer 1782 turned back an American force on the Combahee River—one of the last engagements of the war.

ROYAL ARTILLERY

W e typically think of the British as "Redcoats" and the Americans as "Bluecoats" during the Revolution. Some units, though, wore the opposite colors.

The British Royal Artillery, for example, wore blue regimental coats with red facings. Might they be confused with their colonial foes, amid the thick smoke of battle? Not likely. The artillery were usually aligned well behind the combat troops, away from close-range fighting. They directed heavy cannon fire against the distant enemy, often before the infantry or cavalry soldiers entered the fray.

The "modern" Royal Artillery dates to 1716, when two companies were established at Woolwich (greater London). Woolwich today remains the home of the regiment.

Four battalions made up the 18th-century Royal Artillery. Each battalion contained at least eight companies, and each company consisted of 116 men. Besides the officers, an artillery company had 18 gunners. Most of the men in the unit were apprentice gunners. These apprentices helped man the big guns and also guarded the entourage. For this role, they were armed with light flintlock rifles.

Who drove the horse teams that pulled the heavy armament from one position to another? Interestingly, King George's army usually hired civilians for this task. So a lot more was involved in artillery warfare than simply aiming a cannon and igniting a charge. An artillery company was well-organized, well-trained, and hard-working.

One entire battalion of the Royal Artillery and part of two others were sent to America during the Revolution. They served throughout the colonies, wherever heavy bombardment was required.

BUTLER'S RANGERS

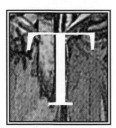

The Americans who remained loyal to the British Crown during the Revolution, called Tories or Loyalists, were invaluable to King George's military effort. Tories were effective—and sometimes ruthless—fighters throughout the colonies. They were feared and hated by American Patriots, who were often the Tories' neighbors in civilian life. When Patriot soldiers knew Tories were among the opposing forces, they fought with greater passion.

Lt. Col. John Butler's ranger unit consisted of frontiersmen, experienced in the way of the woods. Their mission on behalf of the British army was "to serve with the Indians as occasion shall require." Based at Fort Niagara, New York, their main role was to raid the frontier in upper New York State.

Butler's Rangers are remembered best for the 1778 Wyoming Valley Massacre along the Susquehanna River in northern Pennsylvania. Some 400 of Butler's men and 500 Indian allies captured several American blockhouses, mutilated the captured militia, then began destroying patriot homesteads in the valley. They took more than 200 scalps. The bodies of the Tories' victims were said to have "infested the border of the Susquehanna as low as Shamokin."

After a brutal follow-up raid by Tory rangers and Indians in New York's Cherry Valley, the American general John Sullivan was sent with 4,000 soldiers to retaliate. They burned dozens of Indian settlements and destroyed croplands.

Butler's Rangers served until the end of the Revolution. Most of them then relocated to Upper Canada with their families. Butler, a farmer before the Revolution, returned to the fields until his death in 1796.

HESSE-CASSEL JAGER CORPS

They were hunters—literally. The ancient German word *jaeger* (the *j* is pronounced as *y*) means "huntsman" or "to hunt." In their German homeland, men of the Jager Corps had been experienced, often well-to-do foresters and hunters of wild game. In America, they wore green and their "prey" was the Continental army. They were the Crown's counterpart to the feared American frontier marksmen who were demoralizing British ranks with their long rifles.

Most Jagers were armed, not with long rifles, but with their own private muskets or rifles, with which they had become expert shots before the war. They were mostly skirmishers. Their task was to pick off as many American soldiers as possible before the opposing lines of infantry closed ranks. Well-disciplined, they were put to excellent use. Their favorite targets were Bluecoat officers.

Though best employed as marksmen from a distance, they sometimes had to fight at close quarters. They carried small hunting swords for hand-to-hand combat. Most Jagers were foot soldiers, although one mounted company also took part in the Revolution.

Jagers were organized in small units (usually no more than 30 men). It's estimated that fewer than 1,000 Jagers served in the Revolution, though they were in great demand by the British commanders. They began arriving in New York in mid-1776 and served as far south as Savannah, Georgia. In the siege of Charleston, they were especially useful as snipers protecting British trenching engineers.

REGIMENT PRINZ FRIEDRICH

The Regiment Prinz Friedrich was one of many units raised from the Brunswick region of north-central Germany and sent to fight for the British in the American colonies. The regiment sailed from its homeland in February 1776. Like many other German mercenary regiments, its destination was Quebec. It arrived after a transatlantic ordeal of more than three months and became part of the British general John Burgoyne's army.

"Gentleman Johnny" Burgoyne's invasion of New York from Canada brought encouraging news to London in summer 1777. Victories at Fort Ticonderoga and Hubbardton led British Loyalists to believe the war would be over soon. But they were sobered by reports of the retreat at Bennington (in present-day Vermont) and the bloody stand-off at Bemis Heights. Survivors of Bemis Heights told horror stories of timber wolves that came to feed by night on wounded soldiers abandoned in the battlefield.

Then came Saratoga, where Burgoyne was forced to surrender practically his whole army. The king and Parliament had to acknowledge victory would not come soon—if at all.

Most of the Regiment Prinz Friedrich were taken prisoner at Saratoga. Some, though, returned to service in Canada, assigned primarily to garrison duty.

The musketeers used firearms different from ordinary rifles. Their muskets could be loaded with more than a single ball. Indeed, rebel musketeers were hated by the British because they often loaded their weapons with half a dozen balls of different sizes.

The Regiment Prinz Friedrich wore dark blue coats with yellow facings.

REGIMENT PRINZ LUDWIG

he Regiment Prinz Ludwig is believed to have been the only German horse regiment to fight in the Revolutionary War—and it fought on foot, for the most part. When the regiment arrived in Quebec in summer 1776, the soldiers expected to obtain horses and equipment locally. Imagine their dismay to find very few mounts available in the colonies.

Actually, that may have been just as well. Many of the battles of the American Revolution were fought over obstructed terrain, where cavalry would have been unable to charge. Mounted units were useful mainly for scouting and raiding missions.

Dragoons were noted for their especially heavy equipment among European armies of the day. They carried formidable broadswords. Historians have wondered whether the men of the Regiment Prinz Ludwig kept their heavy cavalry boots after they became foot soldiers; some believe they exchanged them for lightweight infantry gaiters—much more practical for forced marches and field combat.

Like many other German units, the regiment took part in Gen. Burgoyne's ill-fated New York campaign of 1777. In August of that year, many of the men were killed at the Battle of Bennington, where the Germans were turned back by a valiant colonial effort. The rest were captured two months later at Saratoga, New York. However, the regiment was able to regroup after some of the men were exchanged for American prisoners of war; they were joined by comrades who managed to escape from captivity.

The Regiment Prinz Ludwig dressed in light-blue coats with yellow facings.

REGIMENT VON DITFURTH

he British army, although highly disciplined and efficient, was vastly outnumbered in the War of Independence. The regular British army probably consisted of fewer than 50,000 soldiers at the time of the war. By contrast, one source estimates that there were almost 500,000 potential fighting men in America (though some of them were Tories supporting England).

England turned to Germany for support. About one-third of the British army in America consisted of German auxiliaries. Germany during the 18th century was known for providing Hessian soldiers to different military causes throughout Europe. These mercenaries—professional troops whose loyalty was for sale—were known, on occasion, to join opposing armies and fight against each other.

Some Germans were shipped to Quebec to join Burgoyne's army in 1776. But the Regiment von Ditfurth was sent to New York and engaged in the campaign for control of Long Island under British commander Sir William Howe. It was a glorious time for the Redcoats and their Hessian allies, who defeated Washington's patriot troops on Long Island and captured New York City.

But the Continental army, though defeated, escaped potential destruction on Long Island. The war moved into New Jersey and Pennsylvania, and the Americans began scoring notable victories. Among them was Gen. George Washington's humiliating surprise capture of a large Hessian force at Trenton, New Jersey, on Christmas night 1776.

The Regiment von Ditfurth was eventually transferred to the southern colonies. It took part in the successful siege of Charleston late in the war.

REGIMENT VON RHETZ

Thousands of German Hessians fought for the British in the American Revolution. Though these men were fighters for hire, the princes of their home districts—not the soldiers themselves—got most of the pay and benefits for their efforts. Hessians were formidable warriors, especially skilled with the bayonet in hand-to-hand fighting. Soldiers from the Hesse-Cassel region were considered the best prepared of the German units.

The Regiment von Rhetz had been raised in 1748 and was sent to Canada in summer 1776. The men of the grenadier infantry battalion were chosen because they were exceptionally tall and strong. They often formed the reserves in conflicts, held back until a critical moment when their entry would prove decisive.

The regiment joined Gen. John Burgoyne's invasion of New York State from Canada in 1777. Burgoyne (who, surprisingly, was a playwright in civilian life) captured Fort Ticonderoga in July of that year. He hoped his campaign would break the back of the Continental army and end the Revolution. Instead, the invasion ended in Burgoyne's infamous defeat three months later at the hands of the American general Horatio Gates at Saratoga, New York. The Regiment von Rhetz was captured, along with most of Burgoyne's army.

The Regiment von Rhetz wore dark blue coats with white facings.

An interesting footnote regarding the Hessians is that by the end of the war, a few had "turned coat" and become fighting Patriots. And among those who had remained loyal to the Crown, many settled in America after the peace treaty and became part of the American tapestry.

2ND REGIMENT OF CONTINENTAL LIGHT DRAGOONS

When Gen. George Washington pleaded for more soldiers in 1776, four regiments of light dragoons were raised to join the Continental army. The first of these regiments, commanded by Col. Elisha Sheldon of Connecticut, became the 2nd Continental Light Dragoons. It served for the length of the war.

A light dragoon regiment consisted of about 400 soldiers. Traditionally, dragoons were among the most heavily armed and most feared cavalrymen of 18th-century armies. But the art of war was becoming more complicated—especially on the American continent, where the terrain, overall strategies, and actual battle tactics called for new methods of fighting. Light dragoon units were more maneuverable and gave army commanders more flexibility in laying their plans.

The 2nd Regiment of Continental Light Dragoons patrolled primarily in New York and New England during the war. But they were also at the dreadful American defeat at Brandywine Creek, Pennsylvania, in 1777 and were in on the great victory at Yorktown, Virginia, four years later. Meanwhile, they had operated a valuable network of American spics and taken part in successful coastal raids around New York City and Long Island.

The four light dragoon regiments chose very different uniforms. The 2nd was the only one to wear blue coats at the beginning of the war; the coats had buff-colored facings. The 1st Regiment initially wore brown but eventually also took blue coats, with green facings. The 3rd Regiment wore white, and the 4th wore green (after beginning service decked out in red coats captured from the British).

4TH MASSACHUSETTS REGIMENT

The term *light infantry* indicated a military unit that was armed with lighter and less powerful weapons than grenadiers. The men wore lighter clothing. The term also indicated that the soldiers were smaller in stature. Organizing a unit of this kind was suggested after the British suffered an important defeat during the French and Indian War, 20 years before the Revolution. Mobile forces like these could be decisive in certain situations.

Today's sophisticated weapons can be operated by a soldier or sailor of almost any size. Commandos, increasingly important in late 20th-century combat, might be either large and brutish or small and nimble. It's puzzling for us to think of whole military units as "light" or "heavy." But in the 1700s, when forced marches and bloody hand-to-hand infantry encounters were common tactics, physical size often determined the type of unit a soldier would join. And it often determined the outcome of a battle.

Light infantry were not necessarily less important than grenadiers. They simply served a different purpose. Regular infantry were usually maneuvered to the center of battle lines. The quicker light infantry were ideally positioned on the flanks. If they could encircle the enemy army, strike from the rear, and pin the opposing ranks in crossfire, victory was usually assured. They were also dispatched as skirmishers, harassing the enemy lines before the main armies closed ranks.

The Light Infantry Company of the 4th Massachusetts Regiment, assembled late in the war, was said to be one of the Continental army's best-outfitted units. The men wore peaked helmets and hunting shirts fringed in linen. The officers were armed with only swords and short spears.

6TH VIRGINIA REGIMENT, CONTINENTAL LINE

The 6th Virginia was among many regular army units raised in early 1776 by order of the Continental Congress. The regiment's men provided their own hunting shirts, typically gray with red collars.

It proved difficult to attract men to the regular army. One reason was that individual colonies were raising militias to defend their homelands. A settler or frontiersman could join a militia company and expect to serve only when needed and within the borders of his home colony. Regular army enlistment, in contrast, meant long-term service, perhaps far afield. Besides, the militia were often paid better. At one point, Virginia offered a $750 bonus plus property to its militia enlistees. For the regular army, Congress authorized only $6.67 a month in pay, and sometimes the pay might be withheld for months.

Nevertheless, the men of the 6th Virginia Regiment, like many others, decided to join the regular army. They were assigned at first to the Southern Department, but in September 1776 they transferred to the main army, and soon they saw action as far from home as northern New Jersey.

Their patriotism was heightened by a wise choice the Continental Congress had made—selecting George Washington of Virginia as the army's commander. Representatives from the northern colonies reasoned that the struggle with Great Britain could not be won without the aid of the South. By choosing Washington to lead the army, the Congress drew vital political and military support from Virginia and the Carolinas.

AMERICAN MILITIAMEN

We remember them as the "Minutemen." They were American colonists, mostly farmers and tradesmen, determined to resist British domination in the mid-1770s. But they were unwilling to commit to service in a regular army—British, independent, or otherwise. Instead, they volunteered to serve their home colony, as the need arose, pledging to be ready to fight at a minute's notice.

The most famous militia, the Massachusetts Minutemen, became the first to engage the British in actual combat. The fighting occurred April 19, 1775, at Lexington, 12 miles northwest of Boston. The British sent 1,800 soldiers inland to destroy a large supply of weapons the troublesome militia had been storing and to capture leaders of the independence movement. Their mission was secret, for its success hinged on surprising the colonials. They left Boston by night.

But watchful Americans known as the Sons of Liberty sent three men—Paul Revere, a silversmith; William Dawes, a shoemaker; and Samuel Prescott, a doctor—to raise the militia. The British found 70 Minutemen waiting for them at Lexington Common early on the morning of the 19th. A shot was fired—history is unclear whether by an American or a Redcoat—and the common was soon enveloped in musket smoke from both sides. The militia dispersed, leaving eight men dead.

A more significant skirmish occurred later that day at Concord, five miles farther inland. Though neither action was important strategically, together they marked the beginning of the Revolutionary War.

American militia fighters usually wore no formal uniforms and used their own firearms.

AMERICAN RIFLEMEN

When we read of historical battles, we usually assume the army that won had more soldiers or more and better equipment or smarter leaders or better training. Or its fighters were simply braver and better than their opponents.

But countless other factors could give the real edge to a unit that was smaller, weaker, and more frightened than the enemy. A sudden change in the weather, for example, might slow the progress of an army maneuvering frantically for position, while having little effect on its foe.

And what if the opposing forces were armed differently? There were times when a bayonet was useless—and other times when it was the most important weapon on the field.

In the colonies, British troops encountered a new kind of soldier. The riflemen of Pennsylvania, Maryland, and Virginia were often clothed in buckskin and fought with a different type of gun. Their "long rifles" were accurate at great distances. The men who fired them had precise aim, acquired during years of hunting wild game for food. They could regularly hit enemy targets more than 100 yards away—far out of range of British musket fire. Moving from tree to fence post to rock for cover, they could take down Redcoat officers in the distance before the infantry troops even began fighting. They were also especially useful in protecting remote outposts plagued by Indian attacks.

But the frontier riflemen were poorly equipped for close combat. It took longer for them to reload than it took musketeers, and long rifles could not be fitted with bayonets.

Riflemen were an American contribution to military tactics. They brought a deadly frontier skill to the battlefield.

GREEN MOUNTAIN RANGERS

E than Allen, one of America's favorite heroes of the War of Independence, commanded the Green Mountain Rangers, better known as the "Green Mountain Boys." They were settlers from New Hampshire and what would become Vermont. Like Davy Crockett and Daniel Boone, Allen had a reputation for strength and courage on the frontier, for fighting bears with only a knife.

His rangers, formed soon after fighting began in 1775, were angered over a long-standing dispute in which the king's governors deeded much of their land to Loyalists from New York. They eagerly followed Allen—declared an outlaw by the royal government as a result of the disputes—in the capture of Fort Ticonderoga from the British.

Fort Ticonderoga overlooked the western shore of Lake Champlain, across from the rangers' home territory. In a surprise night attack, they slipped inside the fort and took it in approximately 10 minutes. When blinking British officers demanded to know in whose name these strangers fought, Allen thundered, "In the name of the Great Jehovah and the Continental Congress!"

A month later, the Green Mountain Boys were among the Americans forced to retreat from Bunker Hill in Massachusetts. Allen, known for his brash decisions and his ego, did not continue as their leader. The Green Mountain Boys elected the even-tempered Seth Warner—a friend of Allen's—as their commander.

Even to their allies, the Green Mountain Boys were known as "wild people." Early in the war, they wore ordinary work clothing and hunting shirts. Later, they adopted green uniform jackets but continued to wear buckskin trousers.

Haslet's Delaware Regiment

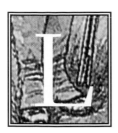

L ike most soldiers in the Continental army early in the Revolution, the men of Col. John Haslet's Delaware Regiment signed up to serve their homeland for just one year. Their unit was formed in December 1775—seven months before the colonies declared themselves independent. The soldiers assumed that by the end of 1776 the conflict would be over and they could resume civilian life.

But 1776 ended with the colonies in dire straits. Haslet's men had suffered along with the rest of General Washington's army in the dismal evacuation of Long Island and New York City. They had earned a reputation as an outstanding regiment within the Continental army, excellently led by Haslet. They distinguished themselves especially well in defending Chatterton's Hill near White Plains, New York.

But most of their actions—even their successes—were part of a general retreat in the face of Britain's professional Redcoat machine. Haslet himself was killed while rallying beleaguered Bluecoats in a furious battle near Princeton, New Jersey, in early January 1777. Washington struggled to hold together a force strong enough to oppose the British.

The Continental Congress ordered new regiments to be raised for the country's defense. Men of the revived Continental army were offered land as additional compensation to keep them fighting.

The Delaware and Maryland units came to be regarded by the end of the war as some of the best fighters of the Continental army.

PENNSYLVANIA LINE

he War of Independence, like European wars of the 18th century, was based on "linear" tactics. Opposing soldiers faced each other in battle lines and (ideally) fired, advanced, and retreated in formation. Americans enlisted in regiments that were being raised within their home colonies. The Continental Congress ordered Pennsylvania to provide 12 infantry regiments to the Continental army in 1776. The 2nd Regiment of the Pennsylvania Line fought from then until the end of the Revolution.

Although battle-hardened and wise, soldiers of the Pennsylvania Line were discontented by the winter of 1780–81. The lot of all Revolutionary War soldiers was generally miserable, as they camped, marched, and fought for months in every kind of weather. The Pennsylvanians—making up a fourth of Washington's army—also resented mistreatment by some officers, unfair compensation, and poor food.

In 1780, their home state began offering better wages plus 200 acres of land to attract new enlistees. Some of these inexperienced but better-paid recruits were criminals released from jail to become soldiers.

A vast body of Pennsylvania soldiers mutinied in January 1781 and marched to confront Congress with their grievances. To resolve the crisis, many mutineers were allowed to be honorably discharged and then to re-enlist. The Pennsylvanians had the sympathy of harshly treated soldiers from other states. A potential mutiny within the New Jersey Line had to be put down and some of its leaders executed.

As the war neared its end, Pennsylvania units continued to serve in Virginia and the lower states. They wore brown dress coats with green facings.

RHODE ISLAND TRAIN OF ARTILLERY

Freedom was in the air, and armed American colonists from throughout New England converged on Boston to make it happen.

It was spring 1775. Rag-tag Minutemen had daringly engaged British regulars at Lexington and Concord, firing the first shots of revolt. Now the Massachusetts patriots were being joined by freedom fighters from Rhode Island, Vermont, and New Hampshire—some 10,000 men in all—to surround the British army stationed in Boston.

Maj. Gen. Artemus Ward, the colonial commander, called his force the "Army of Observation." Their role, he figured, was to ensure that the British did not march inland and harm the independence-minded townships.

But by July, the new Continental Congress had appointed George Washington to replace Ward and become commander-in-chief of the Continental army. Washington saw Boston as an important military objective, and the city was placed under siege. In March 1776, he forced the British to withdraw after secretly moving heavy cannon onto Dorchester Heights above Boston. Sir William Howe's Redcoats were evacuated to Halifax, Nova Scotia.

Many ecstatic colonists thought the takeover of Boston meant the Revolution was over. In fact, it was only beginning. Congress did not even declare the colonies' independence until four months later. The British returned in force, and the Continental army was placed on the defensive.

The 96 men of the Rhode Island Train of Artillery were raised as a unit in 1775 and sent to take part in the Boston siege. Their uniforms were notable for the elaborate helmets, inscribed with the motto For Our Country.

SOISSONNAIS INFANTRY REGIMENT

The Continental army was at its most depressing point while in winter quarters at the beginning of 1778. It built crude shelters at Valley Forge, Pennsylvania. As the British weathered the cold in comparative comfort at Philadelphia, 18 miles away, the Americans huddled in mud-floored cabins, cold, sick, and half starved.

Good news came in February. The French, long-time enemies of the English but too timid to join the colonial cause, had been persuaded to change their minds by the patriots' victory at Saratoga the previous October. They announced their entry into the war as American allies.

The Soissonnais Infantry Regiment joined the conflict two years later, as the war approached its climax. They were with the French army commanded by the Comte de Rochambeau, whose troops landed in Rhode Island and moved down the coast. In late summer and autumn 1781, they marched with Washington's Continentals to Yorktown. There, aided by the Comte de Grasse's French navy in the Chesapeake Bay, the allies defeated Lord Cornwallis's Redcoats. This victory decided the outcome of the Revolution, although battles and skirmishes continued for another year.

A fusil was a type of musket; the French word *fuisil* referred to the steel of a flintlock firearm. The Soissonnais fusiliers wore the new French uniform, which called for white jackets; their regiment chose light crimson facings.

French soldiers were ridiculed by the British because of their flashy uniforms—especially when compared with the battered Continental army, many of whom wore dirty, ragged shirts and no coats at all. But the French were outstanding fighters, and their help was critical to the American cause.

CHRONOLOGY

April 19, 1775   Fighting begins at Lexington and Concord, Massachusetts.

June 17, 1775   The British take Bunker Hill (Breed's Hill) outside Boston.

July 3, 1775   George Washington is appointed commander of the American forces by the Continental Congress.

March 17, 1776   The British are surrounded and forced to evacuate Boston by ship.

July 4, 1776   Delegates from the colonies sign the Declaration of Independence in Philadelphia.

August–November, 1776   Washington's army is driven from Long Island and the New York City area.

December 25–26, 1776   Americans capture a large British force in a surprise Christmas night attack at Trenton, New Jersey.

September 1777   Redcoats win the Battle of Brandywine Creek and score other area victories en route to capturing Philadelphia.

October 17, 1777   Americans under Gen. Horatio Gates capture Gen. John Burgoyne's British army at Saratoga, New York.

Winter 1777–1778   Washington's army weathers a miserable winter encampment at Valley Forge, Pennsylvania.

February 6, 1778	France signs an alliance with the American colonies and joins the war.
June 28, 1778	The Battle of Monmouth Courthouse, New Jersey, is a tactical draw but an important psychological victory for the Americans.
July 3, 1778	Tories and Indians carry out the Wyoming Valley Massacre in Pennsylvania.
May 12, 1780	The British capture the port of Charleston, South Carolina.
October 7, 1780	The Americans win the Battle of Kings Mountain, South Carolina, weakening British control in the lower colonies.
March 15, 1781	Lord Cornwallis defeats Gen. Nathanael Greene's Americans at Guilford Courthouse, North Carolina, but suffers heavy losses and withdraws into Virginia.
October 19, 1781	Cornwallis surrenders to Washington at Yorktown, Virginia, signaling the end of the war.
April 19, 1783	Congress orders Americans to stop fighting.
September 3, 1783	The peace treaty is signed by England and America.

INDEX ✳

FURTHER READING

Bennett, Charles E., and Lennon, Donald R. *A Quest for Glory: Major General Robert Howe and the American Revolution.* Chapel Hill: University of North Carolina Press, 1991.

Bobrick, Benson. *Angel in the Whirlwind: The Triumph of the American Revolution.* New York: Simon & Schuster, 1997.

Buchanan, John. *The Road to Guilford Courthouse: The American Revolution in the Carolinas.* New York: John Wiley & Sons, 1997.

Dann, John C., editor. *The Revolution Remembered: Eyewitness Accounts of the War for Independence.* Chicago: University of Chicago Press, 1980.

Ketchum, Richard M. *Saratoga: Turning Point of America's Revolutionary War.* New York: Henry Holt and Company, 1997.

Langguth, A. J. *Patriots: The Men Who Started the American Revolution.* New York: Simon & Schuster, 1988.

Leckie, Robert. *George Washington's War: The Saga of the American Revolution.* New York: HarperCollins, 1992.

Marrin, Albert. *The War for Independence: The Story of the American Revolution.* New York: Atheneum, 1988.

Smith, Page. *A New Age Now Begins: A People's History of the American Revolution.* Vol. 2. New York: Penguin Books, 1976.

Wright, Esmond, compiler and editor. *The Fire of Liberty.* New York: St. Martin's Press, 1983.